PANDEMIC BLUES

A Collection of Musings and
Expressions of Love & Loss...

Rainbow Phoenix

Rainbow Phoenix Publishing

Twin Flames

Opposites attract, but Twin Flames ignite
With an intensity to engulf everything in sight
My heart, my soul, my reason to exist,
Took my will to live,
Took away my common sense.
Out of the blue, like a bolt,
You couldn't love me anymore.
Just like that. Just like a flash,
A heart trampled on the floor
When she needed him, he was there
But she didn't return the favor.
She turned and ran, cuz she was scared
That he'd do the same to her later.
He opened up his heart, much to his dismay.
He let her in and he played his part,
But now she doesn't feel the same way.
Heart in his hand, lump in his throat,
Wore his love for her on his sleeve.
Plans for a future life together,
Forever- is what she lead him to believe.
Imagine his shock and his surprise,
But it's the story of his life,
He flew too fast, he flew too high
The Damn Universe wins again
No new life, no future wife
That eternal twin flame?
Seems to have reached its end...

Happiness?

Happiness?
What is it?
How do I get it?
And do I even deserve it?
The look of joy upon my face,
Will it ever come to me again?
I had it once before, but suddenly
You decided you needed time
And you needed space
Your heart was no longer mine
Emptiness left in its place.
I thought we were just fine.
What happened?
Why was I evicted?
What did I do?
Where once loved lived,
It's now restricted,
Off limits from now on.
And all those words?
What about their meaning?
Always & Forever- Now Gone.
Gave you my heart,
Gave you my time.
Would give you the Sun and the Stars.
Twin Flames Forever?
Twin Flames Together?
Nope, just alone and apart...

Hurt & Heartbreak

Hurt & Heartbreak
Know no season.
They come and go
Without rhyme or reason.
There is no schedule
For when the darkness starts.
There is no timetable
For a broken heart...

Seasons Change

Seasons change,
Time moves on
They say some people change, too
One thing that's never changed
Was my love for you
Our friendship blossomed into more
As summer turned to fall
But by winter, your love was out the door
Your heart you said you couldn't give
So you left me standing there
Like a tree, who lost it's leaves
Its branches have all gone bare
For our lost love, I grieved
People are like seasons
In the fact that they change
Your heart was torn to pieces
Your love's gone a separate way
Like time, I must move on
For here I cannot stay.
Your love gave me the strength inside
Showed me who I want to be
Your changing gave me the courage
A reason to believe
I can't blame you, I'm not made
Understand Why you had to leave
You're off to change yourself for your family,
Now so I am, hopefully for the better
Maybe our paths will cross again
Hopefully, one day will get together
Unlike seasons or people,
One thing will never change
When I said Always & Forever

When I told you that I loved you
Those words I said were true
My love is not a season
I doesn't come and go
My love will stand the test of time
Even though you're no longer mine.

Trust Issues

I've never really believed that line-
"Call me, if you ever need anything..."
Or the one that goes
"Thank you for helping me, I'll do the same for you..."
Because the truth is, people don't
They're too busy in their own lives
Put my faith in others? I won't.
They don't really have the time.
Its something people just say
To make their guilt go away.
Offers of help often ring hollow
Because the real help doesn't follow
And in despair I'm left to wallow
Always wondering about tomorrow
And about their time, I'd have to borrow
So I turn inward, and hide my sorrow
Knowing the only one I can lean on is me
Their help. I will never see
That's just not how life works for me.
I'm the only one looking out for me.
That's the way it will always be.
Because when I do let people in
And on them I slowly begin
To think that I am able to depend
They only let me down again
And prove that those who call friend
Just disappear the moment when
I need someone to turn to
And lift me out of my solitude
So I just give up even trying
Though inside, I'm slowly dying
For someone to ease this pain
But I can't let them in again
And do this all over for no reason
So they just come and go like seasons
And show me just why I don't believe
That I can trust anyone but me...

11:11

Time flies
Time stands still
Time stops
All this time
So much time
Alone with my thoughts.
Thoughts of her
Thoughts of us
Thoughts of we
Thoughts of the past
Thoughts of the future
Is she thinking of me?
Screenshot and delete
Screenshot and delete
Screenshot
And
Delete
Hour after Hour,
Continuously on repeat.
Space and time
My racing mind
A broken heart
A heart that bleeds
A heart that pleads
Of all her needs
But what about me
I understand
She has a plan
She needs time to heal
She needs space to build
Herself a new life
Because of the strife
That tore the old one apart
She needs the time
She needs the space
Before we can start
Moving forward
Moving toward
A life together
A life that's better
For us both

A life of hope
A life of love
A life of fate
But I must wait
For her to be ready
I must be steady
To be her rock
To be the one
When the time comes
No! Stop!
Don't watch the clock.
Don't send that text
Don't be that guy
Just give her her space
Give her her time
For if you do
Once she is through
Maybe she'll finally come back
Maybe she'll find her way back to you
But what if she's gone for good?

Old Love

Old Love...
Leave Me Alone...
These are the words
From one of my favorite Clapton songs
Twin Flames, you said we were
But now your flame no longer burns...
As I lie here, in this bed alone,
Wondering how I'll ever get back to
A white hot love, that's now gone
"Old Love" blaring from the speakers
And dancing around in my head
Laying alone in this empty bed
Remembering all of the words you said...
"And it's making me so angry...
To know that the flame still burns..."
Clapton softly sings
A "River of Tears" streaming down my face...
Stinging the corners of my eyes,
As the memories still race
Around in circles inside my head
My stomach and my heart both filled with dread...
Music used to be my getaway, my escape.
The music I used to love,
Now fills me with hate-
"Makes me so angry
To know that the flame still burns
Why can't I get over?
When will I ever learn?
Old love..."
Leave...
Me...
Alone...

I Saw Us Today

I saw us today
Except it wasn't you
And it wasn't me
But it was exactly how
I pictured us to be.
Sitting in a restaurant, when
An older couple walks in.
Holding hands across the table
He couldn't take his eyes off her
They seemed so happy together
Like they'd been together forever
As I watched them,
My thoughts turned to you
Wishing I was holding your hand
Back when your love was true
Back when you were
The love of my life,
Back when I was your man.
And you'd eventually be my wife.
Back before you needed time and space
Now I feel like it's your time I waste
Wishing I could hold you again
Instead I hold it all in and pretend
That I dream about us every day.
So many words I want to say.
I saw us again today
Holding hands across the table
I couldn't take my eyes off you
I couldn't, if I wanted to
Except is wasn't you
And it wasn't me
But it was exactly how
I pictured us to be...

When I Get Old

When I get old
I hope I lose my memory
Of this time, that you're not mine
Of this hurt I'm feeling
When I get old
I just hope the things that I do remember
Are the things from this past year-
From July until December
When I grow old
I don't want to know
I don't want to feel this heart break
When I grow old
I only want to remember
The smile upon your face
When I grow old
The only thing I want to remember
Is holding you in my arms, sitting hand and hand
When I grow old
I want to die
With you lying by my side
Knowing that I got to live
With you standing by my side
When I get old and leave this Earth
Returned into the Universe-
If I go first and leave you here
My voice daily, you'll always hear
Saying softly "I love you, dear"
Wiping away all of your tears
When I grow old
I hope that I found
A love like yours and mine,
When you were around
But if I grow old without you

And we don't get back to that time
Or I never get to see your face
Just know that I when I grow old
No one will ever take your place

Erasure

How easy was it to erase all of our memories?
To erase all those things that you said to me
How easy was it to move on?
I looked up and you were gone
All those words and things you said
Messages I daily read
Was your love real, was your love true?
Please tell me this was hard on you
The way it's been hard on me
Messages no longer will I read
The texts and phone calls are now over
8 months of loving under cover
Moving on to your new life
You said you'd be right by my side
Hand-in-hand til the end of time
I was your Always
You were my Forever
Stranded you would leave me, never
Said you would be there for me
When this life I'd finally leave
But now I need you, you're not here
Instead I'm only left with tears
I gave you time, I gave you space
But from my life, you quickly raced
How do I endure this pain
Left me all alone again
Off you went to find your own truth
While I stand here without you
Trying to find my way
I don't know what to do or say
You vowed that you would never leave
I wore my heart upon my sleeve

The strength and love you gave to me
Is now gone, I feel so weak
I'm stuck here, no where to go
I know your life's been hard
Easier I hoped to make it
But that doesn't seem to be in the cards
I guess you could no longer face it
And looking back on all those memories
To move on you had to erase it
Memories of you and me
From me, from my heart
You were taken

Strangers

The moment we first met
I felt us connect
And you said you felt it too
Then we became friends
With an invisible bond, a tether
Our friendship could end? Never!
I always loved you from afar
Held a space deep in my heart
But I could never tell you
I didn't want to ruin it
Didn't want to see our friendship end
But we shared a bond so deep
We shared a bond so true
One day I finally had to tell you-
I told you my hopes
I told you my fears
I told you my dreams
I showed you my tears
I gave you my heart
To you, I bared my soul
You promised to be here
Together, We'd grow old
You let me in
Said we'd still be friends
No matter what happens...
But now you've moved on-
Both love and friendship are gone
Another shot in the gut
But I'm such a dope
For holding out hope
That one day we'll be together
Just a bump in the road

On our path to always
Our path to forever
But I'm still here
And you're still there
We don't even talk any more
I can't look at you
Without feeling blue
Can't think of you and not be sad
Should have kept it inside
I shouldn't have tried...
I could have saved my tears
Would have saved a whole year
A year of sadness and anger
But I tempted Fate
And I learned too late
That we're not even friends
We're just Strangers...

Closing The Door

I guess it's time
To close that door
And finally walk away
I just don't feel
The same anymore
I've got to learn to be okay
With not talking to you
And causing myself
Such pain
While I've hung on
You've moved on
And you're not
Coming back again
Time to close the door
On you,
Time to close the door
On us
Time for me to realize
That we're finally through
Time to pick my heart
Up out of the dust
Time for me
To finally see
That you don't want me anymore
Time for me to realize
You're not walking back
Through that door.
But if and when
You finally do
I'll no longer be here
Because I'm done
Chasing you

I'm shedding my last tear.
You needed time
You needed space
So I just sat here
Running in place.
But you've moved on
Your heart is gone
And I'm alone here,
Spinning my wheels.
I've had a thought
To move off this spot,
It's finally time for me
To break the seal.
To close the door
Lock it and
Throw away the key.
Time for me
To move on from you
The way you've
Moved on from me...

Why Did You Run?

Why did you run?
Why did you hide?
Why do you deny
What we both felt inside?
Always and Forever
Are the words YOU swore
You promised to
Leave me never
You said you loved me MORE
I get it, your life
Was torn all apart
But that didn't mean
You had to take your heart
From me to have your space
To have your time
He stabbed you in the back
When you broke his heart
The love for HIM you lacked
You didn't have to break mine
Now we're also torn apart
Why did you run?
Why is it me you ignore
You said you'd be here
In my time of need
I'll lying here on the floor
But you cannot see
Because I put on a brave face
I hide it well.
So she doesn't know
That I'm running away, as well.
Nowhere for me to go
But here I can't stay
You took back your love

And threw my heart away.
Why did you run?
When I needed you the most?
You said you'd make me whole again
Now your love, your words are just a ghost...

How Did We Get Here?

How did we get from there to here?
How did thinking you go from joy to tears?
How did we go from talking all the time?
How did we go from "You'll Always Be Mine"
How did we lose our "Always and Forever"
How did we lose "I'll never leave you ever?
How did we go from "We'll always be friends"
Is this how it ends,
Never speaking again?
How is it that I was there for you.
Remember when you said
You'd be here for me too?
When I needed you the most
Nowhere to be found,
You're a ghost.
Off building your new life,
Enjoying a life finally free
To be just who you want to be
A life that you promised
Would always include me.
I'm the one who suggested no labels
And loving each other with no timetables
Now the labels are dropped
And the tables have turned
And I'm the one who's left to learn
To live with a heart that's been burned
To try to move on from a love that was spurned

How did I get here?
Where do I go now?
How do I manage to grow now?
When I all ever wanted was you.
To love me the way you promised to.

To hold my hand and say it'll all be okay
To spend my time with you every day.
Damn, I wish I had been stronger
And held on to you just a little longer
Or if you could look at me the way you looked at her.
Or that you'd been honest from the start
And said she was the one who had your heart.
I could have sucked it up and moved on
But instead you gave me hope
And for a few months you turned my life upside down
Made me smile inside, inside and out
Taught me what love was about
And then you took your love away
But promised friends we'd always stay
But it hurts too much to see
You move on without me.
And what you don't even see.
is how I'm dying inside again
Because I lost not just a lover
But I also lost my best friend

My New Necklace

Anxiety around my neck
Like a rope chain made of gold
Hiding what I feel inside
No one can ever know
Depression's haze like a fog
Rolling in so randomly
Weighing on my shoulders & chest
I can barely breathe
I used to be so happy
I used to be carefree
I used to enjoy life
Now what's happened to me?
How did I get here?
How did it all come to this?
Where did it all go wrong?
How long have I been this way?
How long will this go on?
This Anxiety around my neck
Holding my head down
Trying to stay afloat
Trying not to drown
Wish someone would throw a lifeline
And pull me out of this despair
Before this anxiety around my neck
Becomes too much to bear

Lingering

Lingering
Longing
Wanting
Haunting
At night
I pace the floor.
Wishing
Hating
Missing
Anticipating
That you'll
Finally walk back
Through that door.
I steal a glance
I sneak a peak
But I don't want
You to see me
You needed space
You needed time
You needed to be free.
So here I stay
And there you go
Alone and apart
You suffer there
I languish here,
Both with holes
In our hearts.
No other lover
Could ever cover
We used to fit like a glove.
But time and distance
And your resistance

Brought an end to our love
Your heart was shattered
By someone who matter
Yet I'm the one
Who paid the price
I watch from a far
Remembering the scars
Of how things used to be
But if you're suffering
If you're lonely,
Why can't you just
Reach out to me?
For now, we both linger
We both long,
We both pace the floor
Haunted by the love we wanted
But the love we don't have any more
Wishing,
Hating,
Missing
Anticipating
When love will
Finally walk
Back through that door.

A Falling Leaf

A falling leaf
But I'm at peace
Because the sun's still shining
As I sit all alone
Out here on my own
Trying to find me
And just like the sun,
Life does move on
I'm putting you behind me
I thought my world
Had come to an end
Trying to live without you
But I was too blind to see
The world around me
There's so much more to do
Than sit at home
To cry and moan
Because the love you promised
Wasn't true
So I sit alone
Out here on my own
I'm finally at peace
The leaves have replaced the tears
It's been a long year
The highs were high
And the lows were low
But the sun's still shining
As I sit all alone
Out here on my own
Trying to find me
And just like the sun,
Life does move on
I'm putting you behind me

Day Drinking

Day Drinking
Keeps me from thinking
Which keeps me from sinking
Further into my feelings
But the drinking
Still leads to thinking
And drunk thinking
Leaves me reeling
And all up in my feelings
My emotions hit the ceiling
Overthinking
Stop drinking
Stop thinking
Stop this sinking
Turn off my feelings
Stop all this reeling
Can't do this again
Trying to numb the pain
Makes it hurt more
Just close that door
What's it all for?
But I need to numb the feeling
Need to stop overthinking
So I just keep day drinking
And I just keep sinking
It's a vicious cycle...

The Overthinking Overthinker

I make up scenarios
Inside my own head
That fills my insides
Up with dread
It's like I keep
Pulling my own thread
Completely unraveling
To words left unsaid
Because I only do this
To myself
Nobody even knows
This private Hell
Trapped inside
This lonesome cell
To no one else
These secrets I tell
Because I makeup
Scenarios in my own head
I overthink
I need a drink
To quench this thirst
Just makes it worse
Because my head spins
And my whole world ends
These nightmares I create
Destined to become my fate
On you I cannot wait
No one else I can depend
Because I make up
Scenarios in my own head
Filling my insides up with dread
I keep pulling my own thread
Completely unraveling

To words left unsaid
Because I only do this
To myself...

I Had to Let You Go

I had to let you go
It hurt too much
Holding on to a dream
Holding on to us
When so long ago
You moved on
I had to let you go
To get away from the pain
That cut me like a knife
Knowing you didn't feel the same
I had to let you go
It hurt too much to watch
Seeing you move on with your life
Seeing the future that I lost
I had to let you go
I can't even be your friend
Talking to you got my hopes up
That we'd be together again
I had to let you go
There were too many reminders of you
Rain, Rainbows, All our Songs
And the talking owls, too
I had to let you go
It hurt too much
Holding on to a dream
Holding on to us
I had to let you go
So I could finally find me.

The Realization

I don't hate you
But I hate being ignored
I do miss you
And the way things were before
But you're busy with your life
You were able to move on
While inside my head
I couldn't accept you were gone
But you ignore me
And I feel bad
Talking to you
Only makes me sad
It's all one-sided
I'm the one who starts
So I've forced myself
To let you go
To no longer reach out
I won't follow you on social media
I won't attempt to text
Or message you either
I have to learn to accept
That we will never be
That your new life
Does not include me
So I guess it's time for me
To do what I've not been able to
It's time for me to move on
And build a new life
A new life, without You...

Creeping Back

I'm trying
I really am
I don't like feeling this way
Anxiety and depression
Creeping back in every day
I've tried mediation
I've tried audiobooks
I've tried reaching out to friends
But every step forward
Seems to bring 2 steps back
It's like playing Shoots and Ladders
That game was always whack.
I just want to feel normal
I just want to be me again
Back when life was easy
Back when I had friends
Who would listen if I needed
Who would catch me if when fall
Who would pick up the phone
Friends who weren't too busy to call
Friends who kept me from feeling alone
But I'm not here to bash my friends
They have troubles of their own
I just hope none of my friends
Ever feel this much alone.

The Strong Ones

You know what really sucks?
Pretending to be the strong one
The one everyone turns to
The one that gets shit done
Being the problem solver.
Or The Entertainer
The one who has to hide
The fears and tears
And dying inside
"How do you do it?"
"How are you so strong?"
Because I have to
To help you all get along
We make it look easy
So you all can keep going
Our anxiety hidden
Without anyone ever knowing

What's Your Super Power?

You ever notice
When they ask kids
"If you could pick
Any super power,
Which would you pick
And why?"
Nobody ever picks
Invisibility...
Because being invisible SUCKS...
I can see you.
You know that I'm here,
But you don't say a word
And I'm not allowed to.
So we just pretend,
That I don't exist.
Some super power...

Wearing My Heart On My Sleeve

I'm going to lay it out there
Because it's the only way I know to be
I need you to want me
I don't want to be the one you need
I want to fall asleep holding you
And wake-up to see your face
I'm sorry if this seems so forward
But time is something I don't ever waste
I want to be the one who holds you
When life gets a bit rough
And to be the one you turn to
When you feel like giving up
I know we barely know each other
Haven't seen each other in years
But I don't want to do this with another
You help me ease my fears
About what I need to do
So that I can be free
To move on to Chapter 2
The part of life where I start again
Making memories, not planning pretend
Being with someone who makes me happy
And someone who makes me smile
Someone to complete this journey
Someone who makes it all worthwhile
And though I cannot give you the world
I'm handing you my heart
Hoping you will be my girl
Hoping for a brand new start
There's so much to talk about
There's a lot to work out
You have a life without me in it

Your days and nights your own
I can't even give myself to you fully
Only make my thoughts of you known
But if with me, you take this chance
To step out of our comfort zones
And get past our reservations
To conquer our hesitations
To make the life we're both owed
I don't know if we're truly soul mates
But I'm willing to find out
I don't want to continue wandering
I need to erase the doubt
If I finally get the chance
I'll do everything I can
To prove to you
My heart is true
And I deserve to be your man

So This Is Moving On?

I'm not mad
I'm no longer sad
I've got no hard feelings
Towards you
I guess in a way
You could say
That I'm trying to be
Just like you
Trying to move on
Trying to be strong
Trying to find my way
I'm tired of the tears
I'm tired of the fear
I'm tired of being lost
Without you
I'm tired of pretending
Tired of thinking we can be
What we were back then
You wanted time and space
I'm no longer waiting to waste
My time, hoping things change
You're moved on over there
You don't seem to care
That we're not even just friends
You're just someone I know
Someone who chose
To walk out of my life
Done with the anger
The love for a stranger
And a heart full of strife
It's time to find peace
Time for me to see
That I too
Can be happy

Ghost Busting

I want to reach out to you
I feel like I need to say something
But what I don't want to do
Is mess it up and say the wrong thing
I can't afford to put myself out there again
Can't take the chance of being just your friend
It's a lose-lose situation
No way I can win.
If I give in and you're not ready
Then it will only hurt me
So I sit here and say nothing
That's not who I'm supposed to be
I'm not cold and heartless
I really do still care
You're the one who moved on
And left me standing there
What if this was you trying
To get back to being just friends?
Trying to get back to "normal" again
I'm not ready to try,
I'm still not over you
And how you told me goodbye
And how Forever turned into Never
And all the tears I cried
I want to reach out to you
And ask you how you're doing
Ask about your family
But doing will only
Show you're moving on without me
I don't want to know that you're fine
I don't want to see that you're okay
I want to know how you sleep at night

I want to know if you miss me
But why don't you reach out
Why doing you check in on me
When my life was falling apart
Why weren't you here for me?
Wrestling with these thoughts and feelings
Wrestling with my fears
How can I take that next step
When my support has disappeared

Can I do this by myself?
Can I do this on my own?
And if I do this at all
How do I do life all alone?
I want to reach out to you
I want to reply so bad
But I know that if I do
It will only make me sad
Because there's no more You & I
There's no more Beauty & the Beast
No more Albert & Allegra
There's no more you and me
You used to ease my pain
You used to calm my storms
I can't put myself out there again
Knowing that you moved on
So I'll sit here in silence
Messages left on Read
No reply can I provide you
What I want to say left unsaid
I still love you, I still miss you
I remember back to those days
When they weren't just words
That just faded away
You were my flame
You were my twin

You were my one and only
But you needed time
You needed space
You needed to move on without me
I didn't need time
I didn't need space
I had already found myself
I needed you in my life again
I don't want anyone else
You were my hope, you were my dreams
Every time I closed my eyes
But now when I think of you
It makes me want to cry...